SCALES
FOR YOUNG
VIOLISTS

Violin by Johannes Franciscus Pressenda, Turin, 1823
Photos by Justin Robertson
Robertson & Sons Violin Shop, Inc., Albuquerque, NM

©2014
Preludio Music Inc.
Albuquerque, NM

ISBN 1-4706-1928-8

Preludio Music Inc.
exclusively distributed by
Alfred Publishing Co., Inc.
PO Box 10003
Van Nuys, CA 91410-0003

Preludio
Music Inc.

Bowing and Rhythmic Variations

Preparatory Shifts for Foundation Keys

Practice these shifting exercises before each Foundation Key. Play with the top fingerings in first position, then repeat several times with bottom fingering shifts, with and without guide notes.

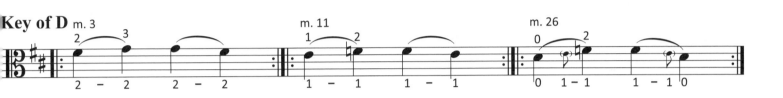

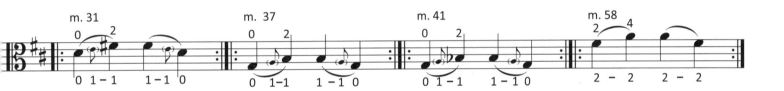

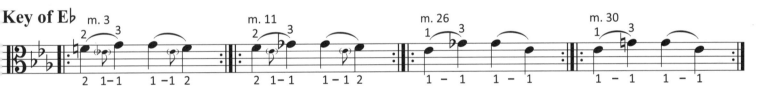

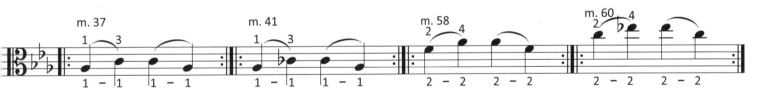

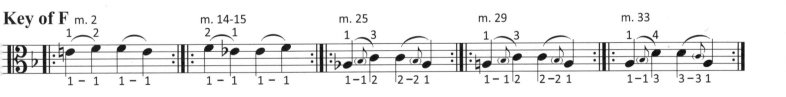

4

Key of G m. 2

Preparatory Shifts for Remaining Keys

Practice these shifts before each key. Play first with the top fingering in the originating or fixed
position, then repeat several times with the bottom fingering shifts, with and without the guide notes.

Key of D♭/C♯ m. 3

Key of E m. 3

Key of F♯

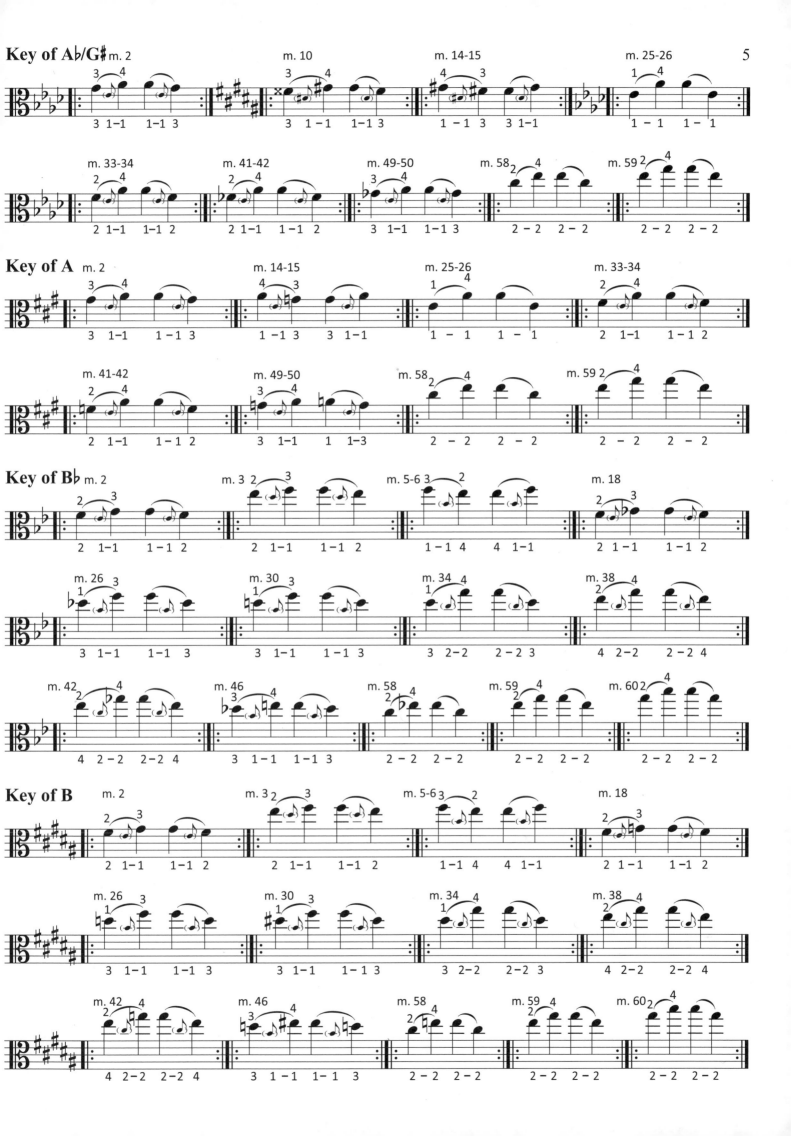

Foundation Key of C

Major

Practice Preparatory Shifts on page 3

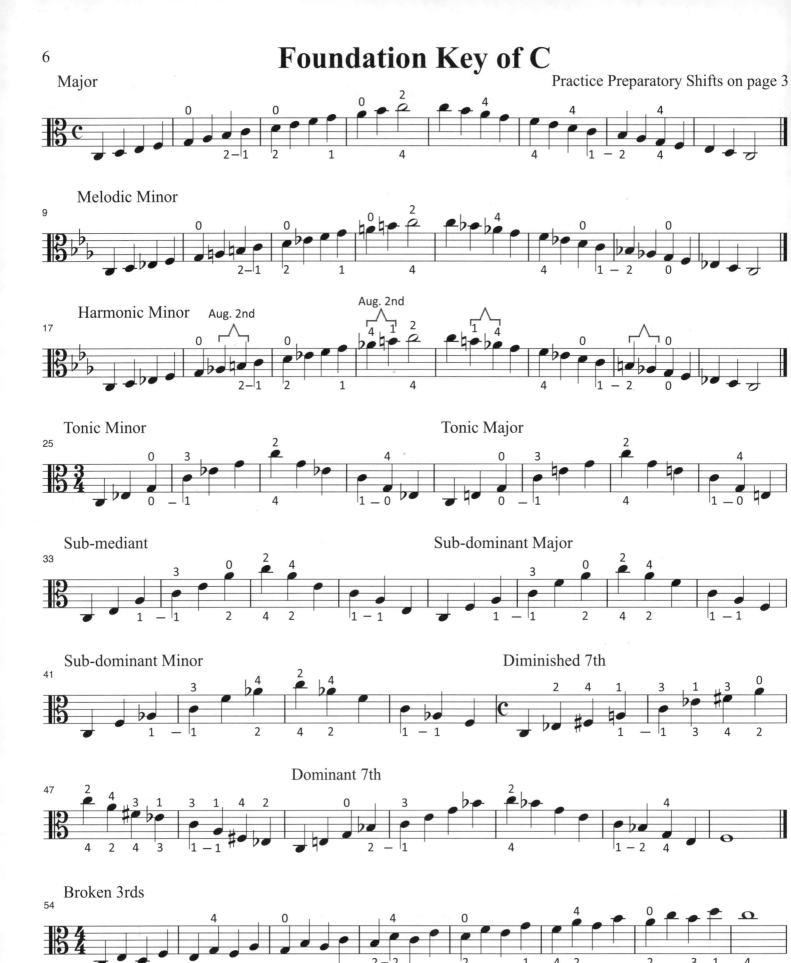

Melodic Minor

Harmonic Minor

Tonic Minor   Tonic Major

Sub-mediant   Sub-dominant Major

Sub-dominant Minor   Diminished 7th

Dominant 7th

Broken 3rds

Chromatic

1st Position Double-Stops

Octaves

Thirds

Sixths

1st-3rd Position Double-Stops

Octaves

Shift 1 & 4 together

Thirds

Sixths

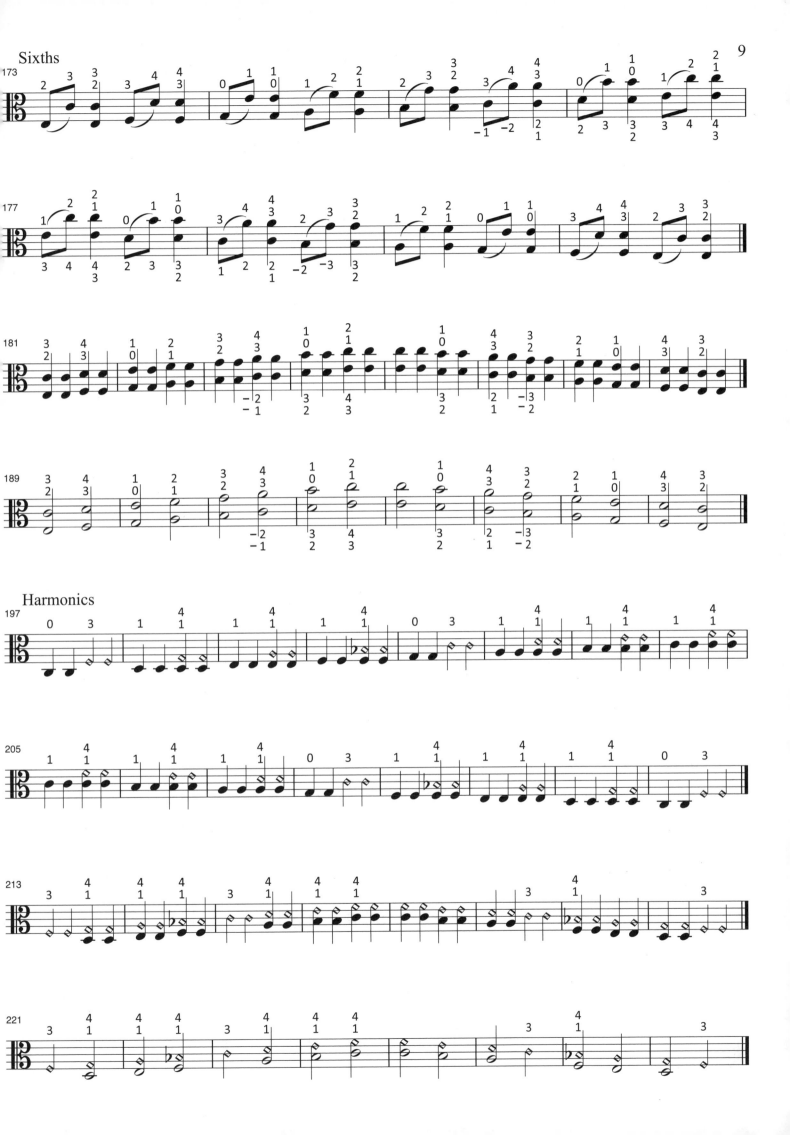

Harmonics

Foundation Key of D

Major

Practice Preparatory Shifts on page 3

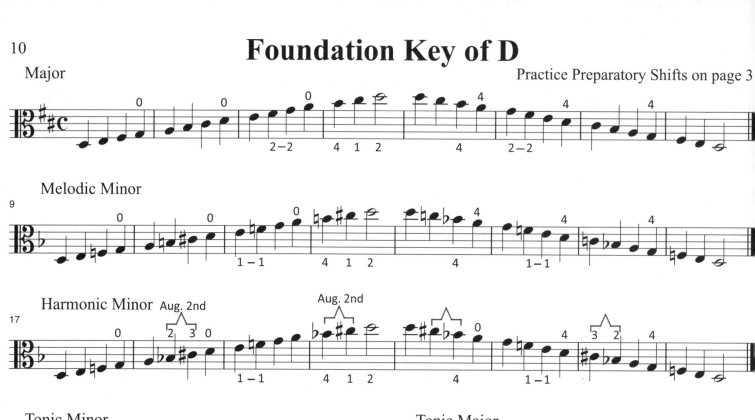

Melodic Minor

Harmonic Minor

Tonic Minor   Tonic Major

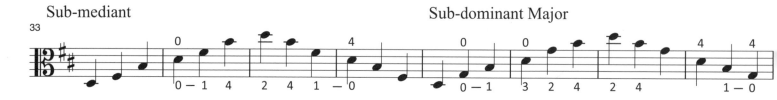

Sub-mediant   Sub-dominant Major

Sub-dominant Major   Diminished 7th

Dominant 7th

Broken 3rds

Chromatic

1st Position Double-Stops

Octaves

Thirds

Sixths

1st-3rd Position Double-Stops

Octaves

Shift 1 & 4 together

Thirds

Sixths

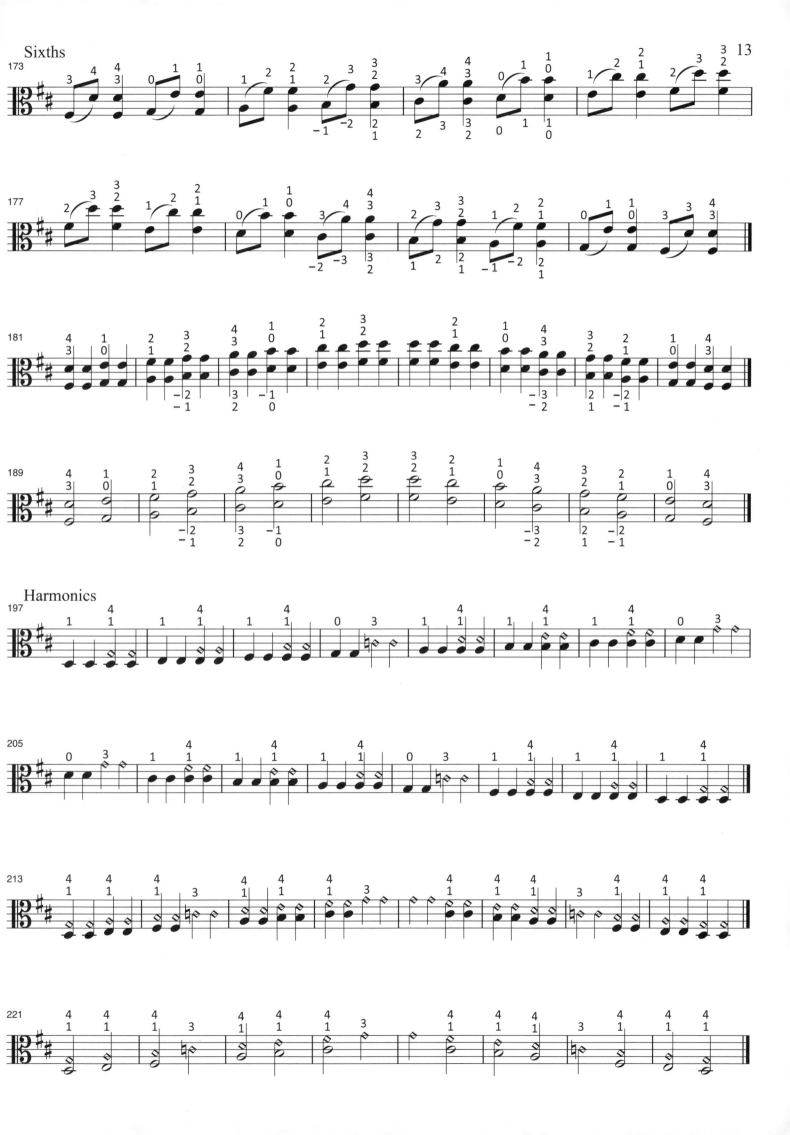

Harmonics

Foundation Key of E♭

Practice Preparatory Shifts on page 3

Major

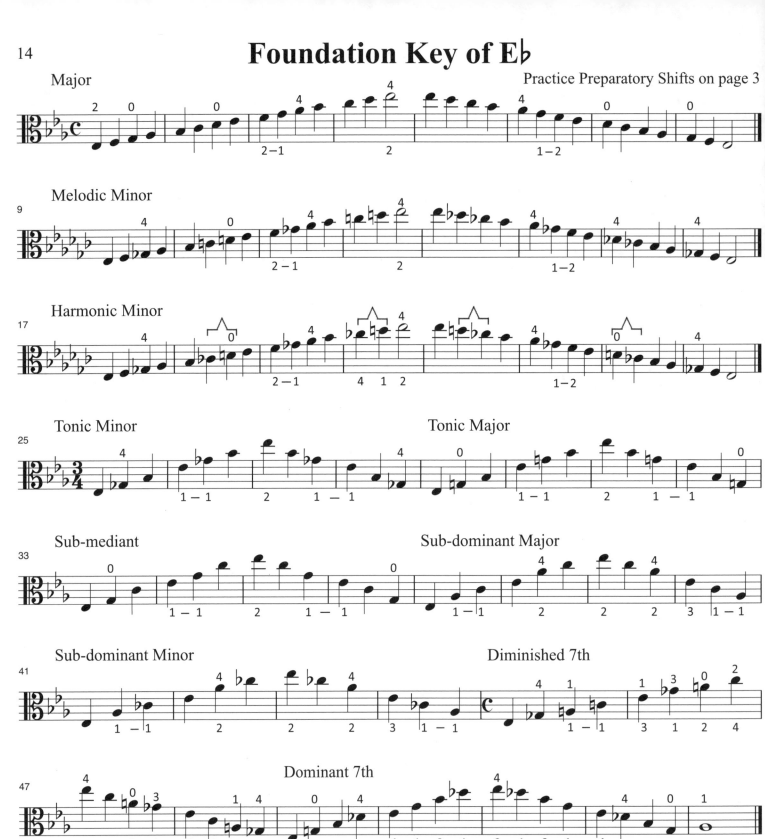

Melodic Minor

Harmonic Minor

Tonic Minor   **Tonic Major**

Sub-mediant   **Sub-dominant Major**

Sub-dominant Minor   **Diminished 7th**

Dominant 7th

Broken 3rds

Chromatic

1st Position Double-Stops

Octaves

Thirds

Sixths

1st-3rd Position Double-Stops

Sixths

Harmonics

Foundation Key of F

Practice Preparatory Shifts on page 3

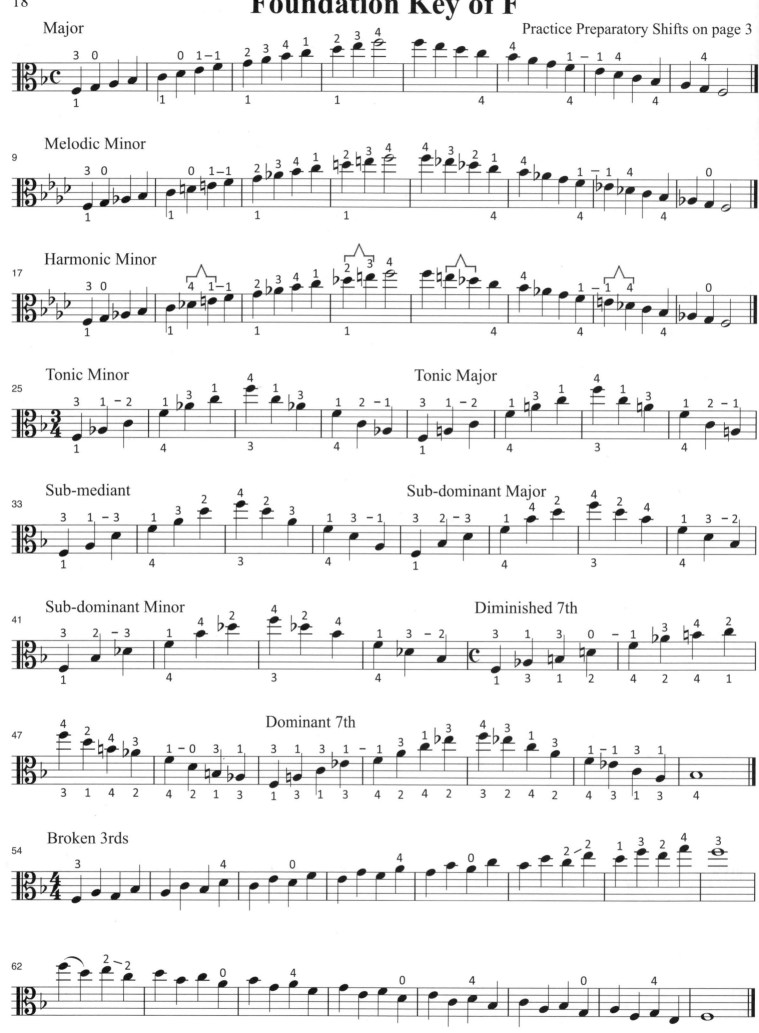

Chromatic

1st Position Double-Stops

Octaves

Thirds

Sixths

1st-3rd Position Double-Stops

Sixths

Harmonics

Foundation Key of G

Practice Preparatory Shifts on page 4

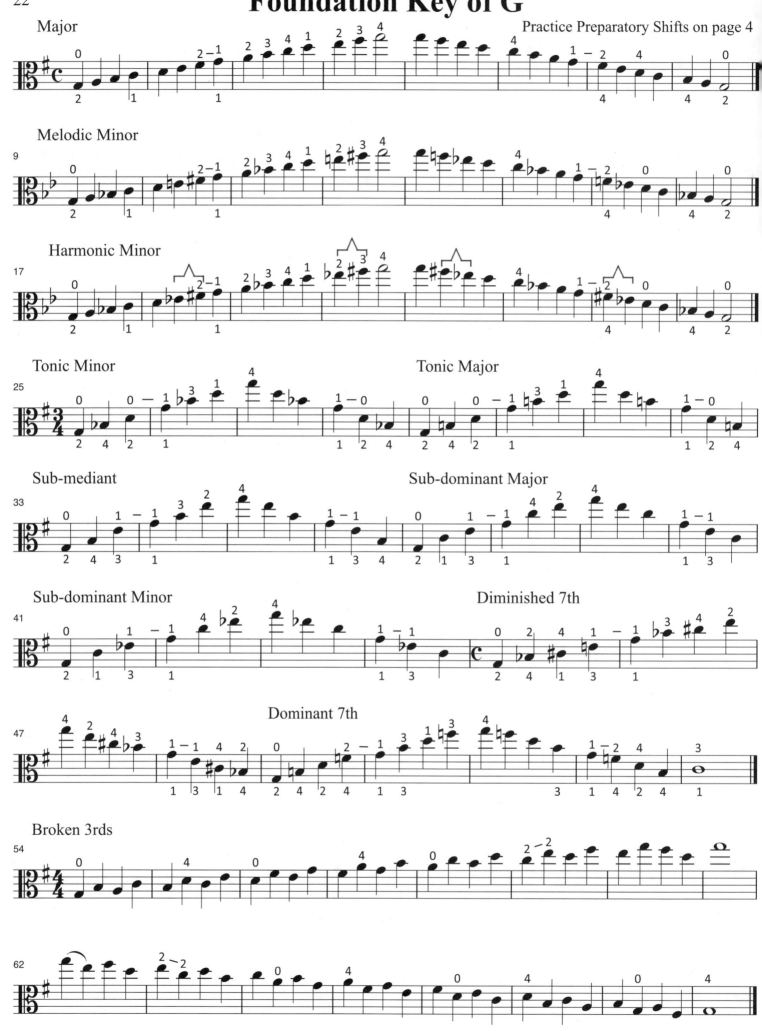

Chromatic

1st Position Double-Stops

Octaves

Thirds

Sixths

1st-3rd Position Double-Stops

Sixths

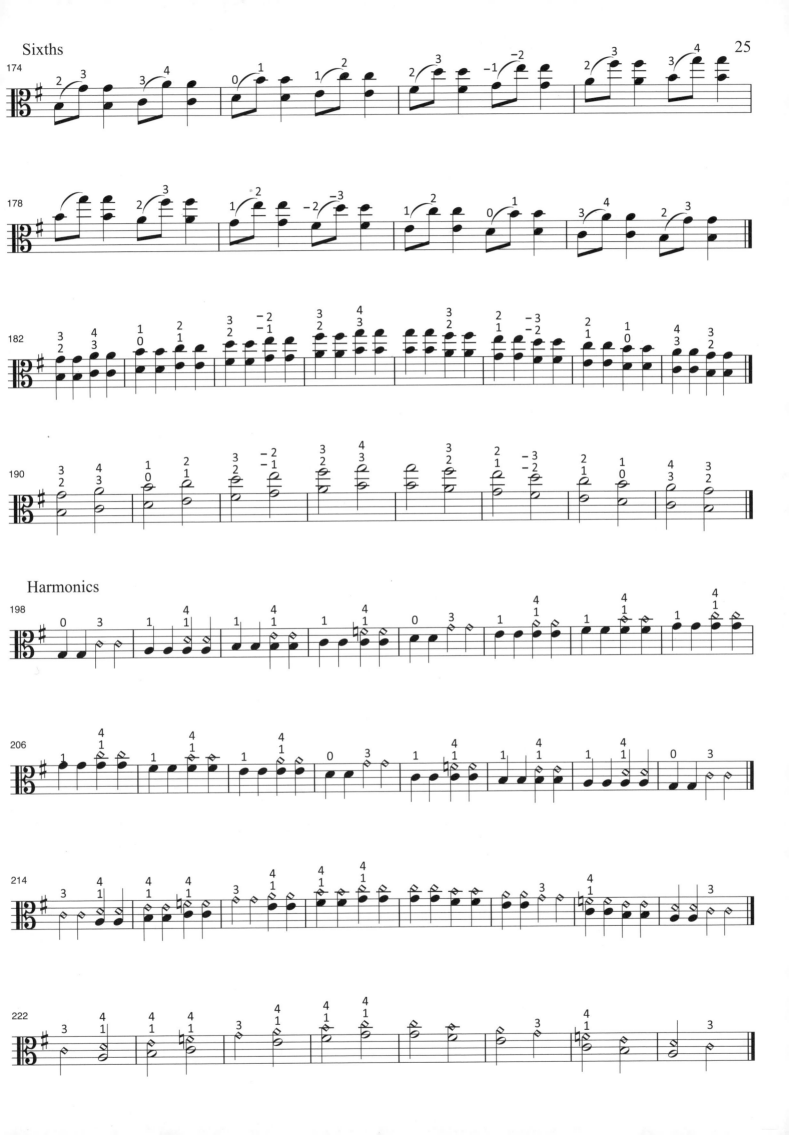

Harmonics

Key of D♭ Major/C♯ Minor

Major

Practice Preparatory Shifts on page 4

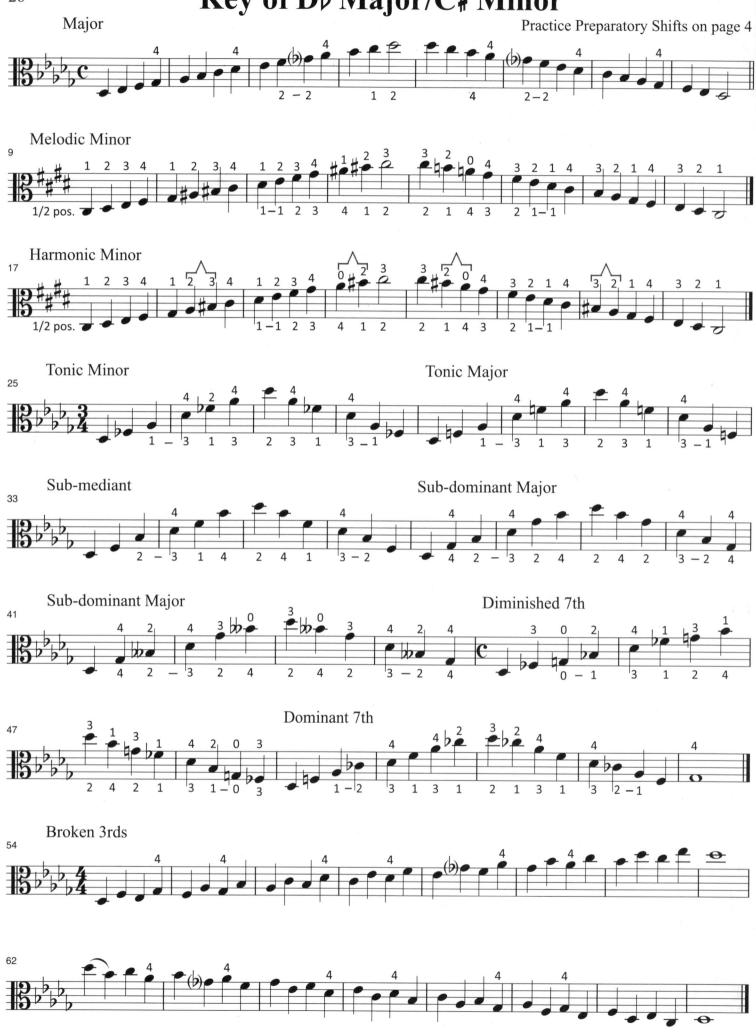

Melodic Minor

Harmonic Minor

Tonic Minor

Tonic Major

Sub-mediant

Sub-dominant Major

Sub-dominant Major

Diminished 7th

Dominant 7th

Broken 3rds

Key of E

Practice Preparatory Shifts on page 4

Chromatic

Octaves

Thirds

Sixths

Harmonics

Key of F♯

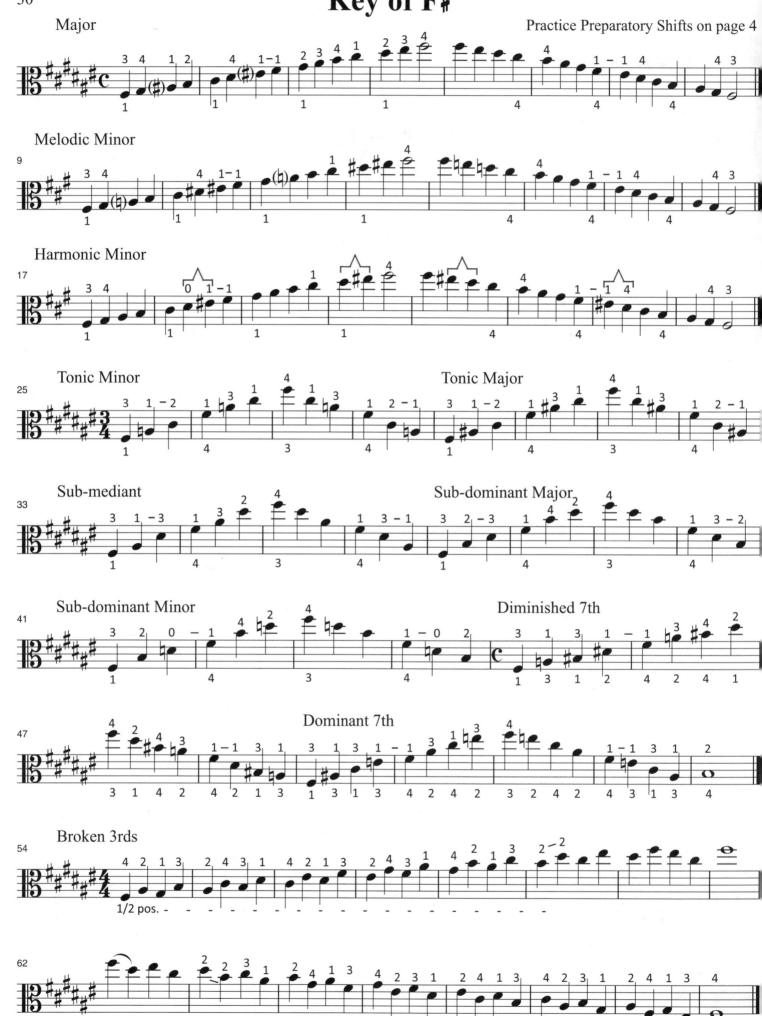

Practice Preparatory Shifts on page 4

Key of A♭/G♯

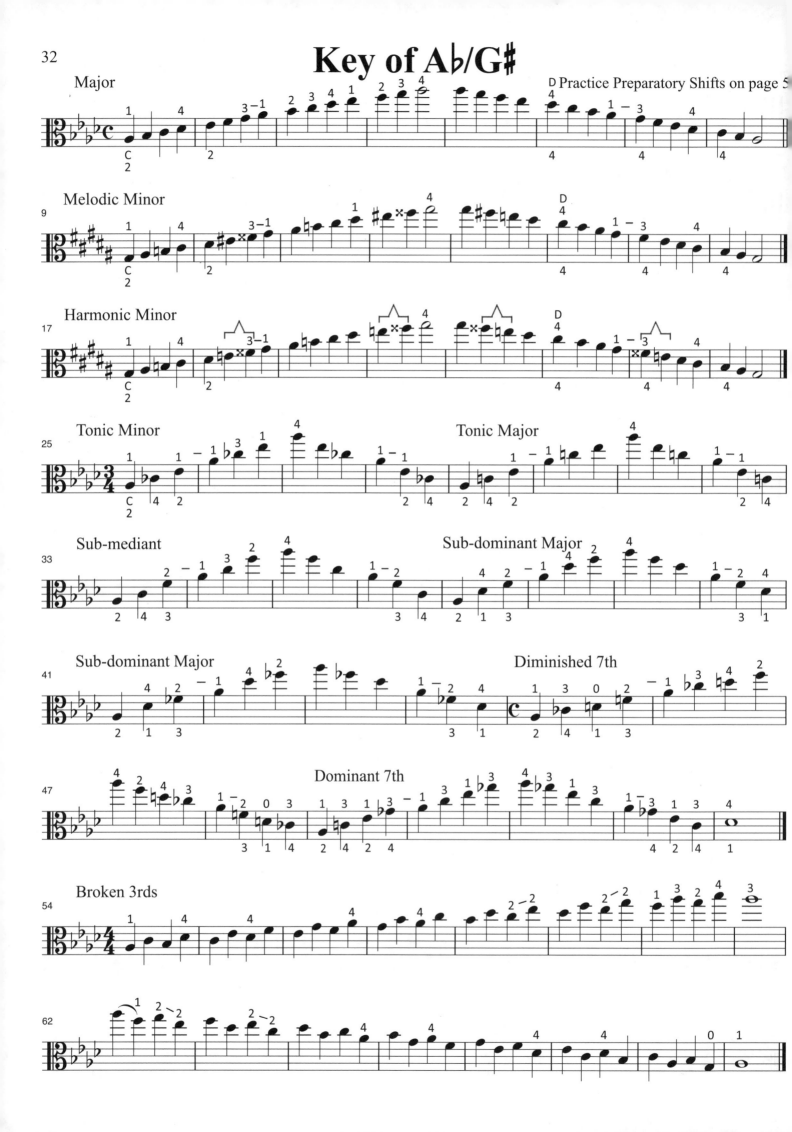

Major

Practice Preparatory Shifts on page 5

Melodic Minor

Harmonic Minor

Tonic Minor — Tonic Major

Sub-mediant — Sub-dominant Major

Sub-dominant Major — Diminished 7th

Dominant 7th

Broken 3rds

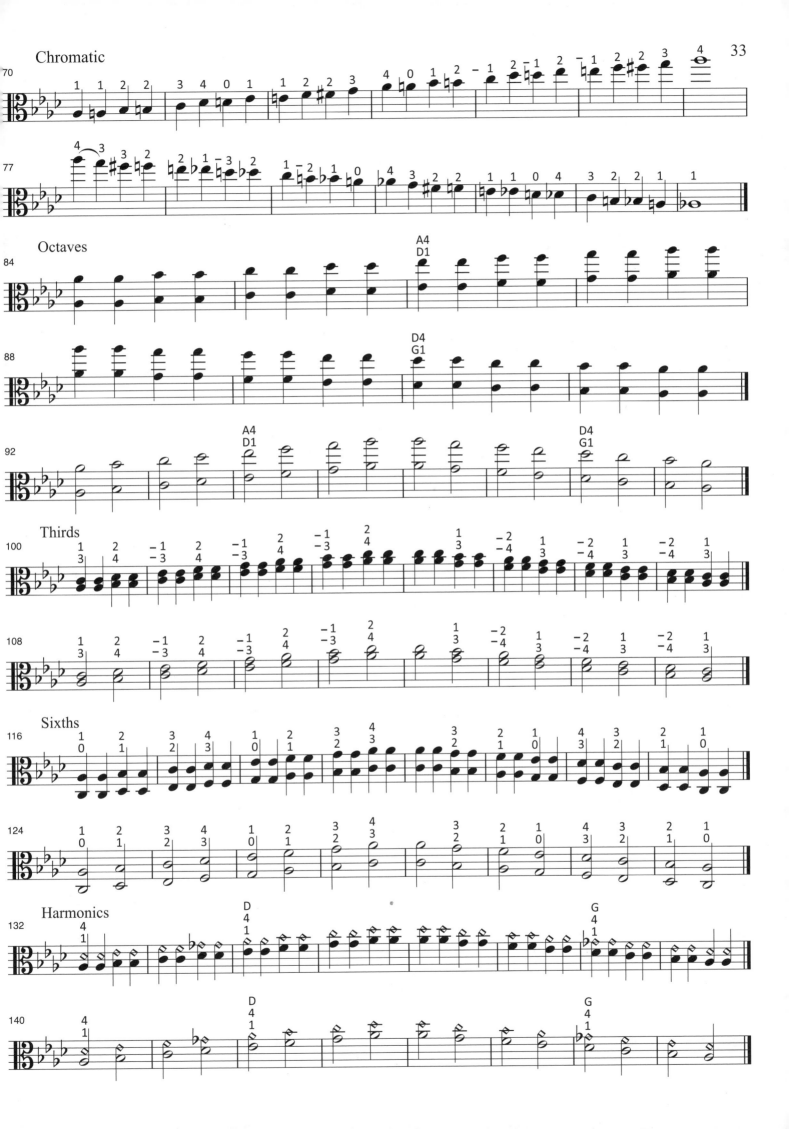

Practice Preparatory Shifts on page 5

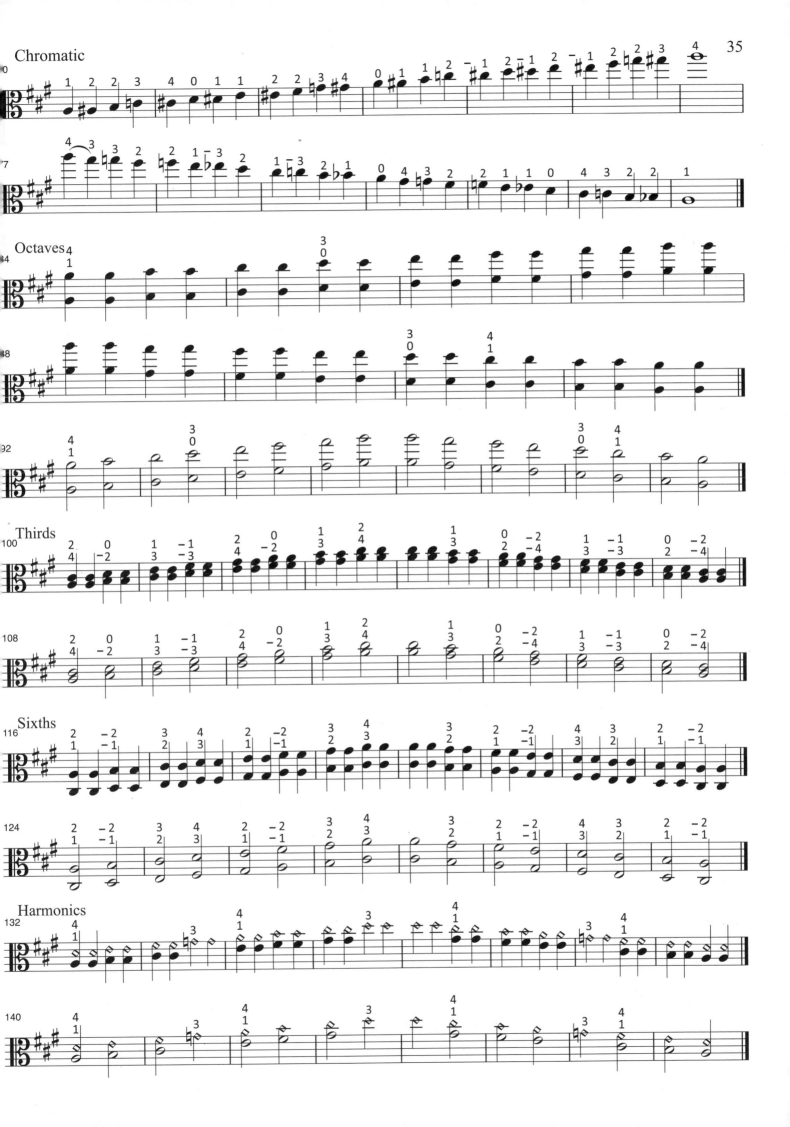

Key of B♭

Practice Preparatory Shifts on page

Chromatic

Octaves

Thirds

Sixths

Harmonics

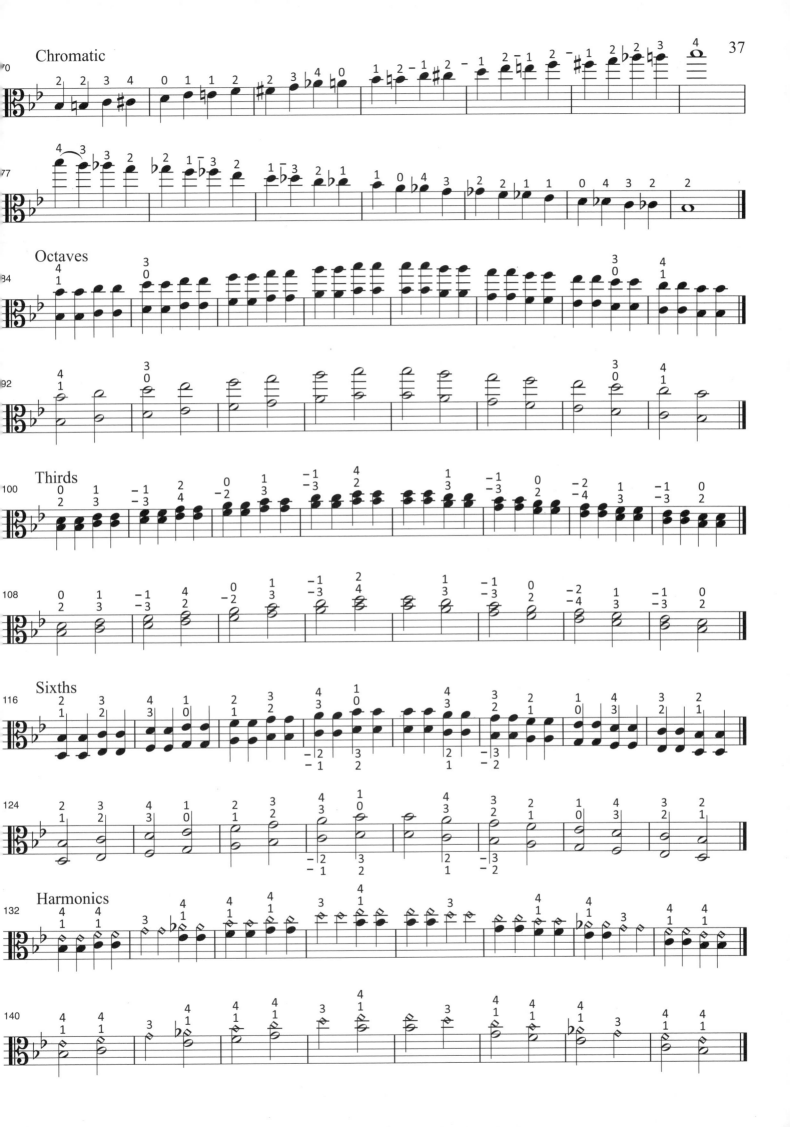

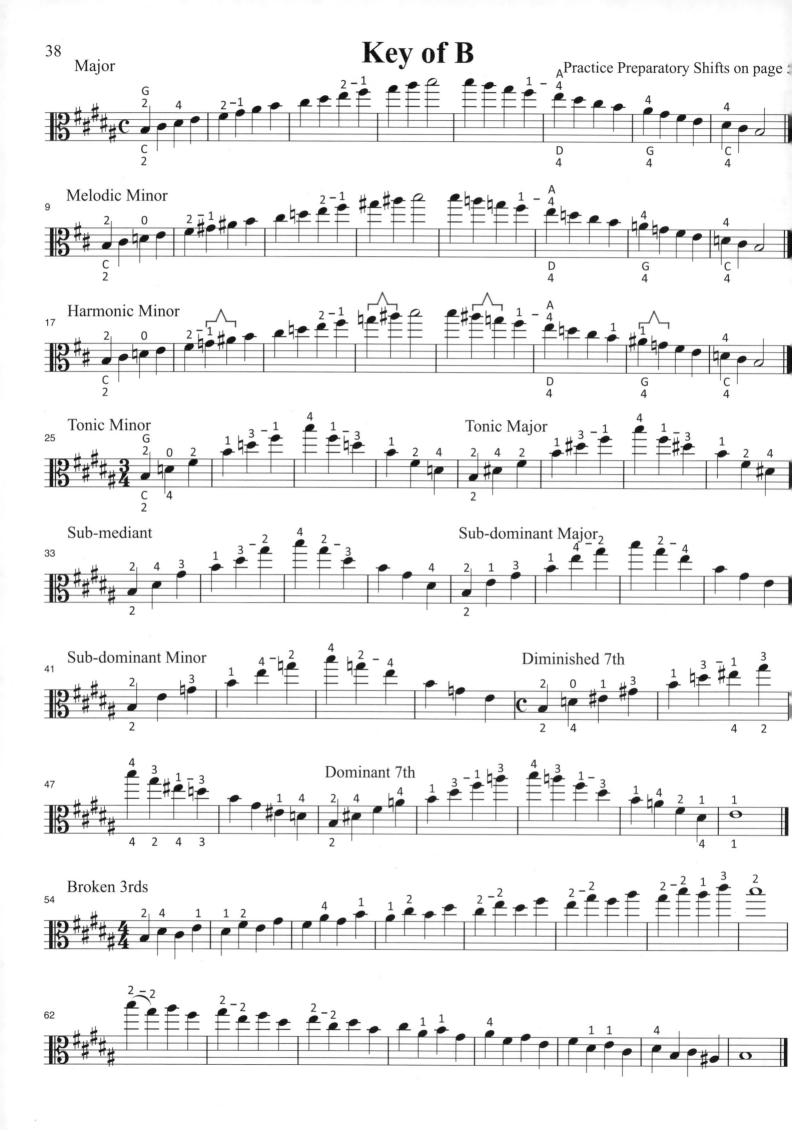

Major

Melodic Minor

Harmonic Minor

Tonic Minor   Tonic Major

Sub-mediant   Sub-dominant Major

Sub-dominant Minor   Diminished 7th

Dominant 7th

Broken 3rds

Practice Preparatory Shifts on page

With more than 40 years of performing and teaching experience, violinist
and violist Barbara Barber joined the sales team at Robertson & Sons
Violin Shop, one of the world's premier bowed string instrument dealers,
in Albuquerque, NM in 2014. Barbara has concertized and presented
master classes and pedagogy clinics across the United States, and in
Canada, Mexico, El Salvador, Brazil, Peru, Colombia, Australia, New
Zealand, Korea, Taiwan, Hong Kong, Japan, Italy, Ireland, Finland,
Sweden and Bermuda. She received her Bachelor of Music and Master
of Music in performance at Texas Tech University with additional studies
at Interlochen Music Camp, Rocky Ridge Music Center, Accademia di
Chigiana in Italy, Taos School of Music and Banff Centre. Barbara has
held faculty appointments at Texas Tech University, Texas Christian
University and the University of Colorado. She has been recognized for
her many articles, presentations and roles on the advisory and editorial
boards of the American String Teachers Association and the Suzuki
Association of the Americas. Barbara's widely-used collections of books
and CDs are published by Preludio Music Inc. and distributed worldwide
by Alfred Music.